W9-AAE-430

SCIENCE EXPLORER

BUGS

SUPER COOL
SCIENCE
EXPERIMENTS:
BUGS

by Susan H. Gray

CHERRY LAKE PUBLISHING • ANN ARBOR, MICHIGAN

CHERRY
LAKE
Publishing

A NOTE TO PARENTS AND
TEACHERS: Please review
the instructions for these
experiments before your
children do them. Be sure to
help them with any experiments
you do not think they can safely
conduct on their own.

A NOTE TO KIDS: Be sure to
ask an adult for help with these
experiments when you need it.
Always put your safety first!

Published in the United States of America by
Cherry Lake Publishing
Ann Arbor, Michigan
www.cherrylakepublishing.com

Content Editor: Robert Wolffe, EdD,
Professor of Teacher Education,
Bradley University, Peoria, Illinois

Book design and illustration: The Design Lab

Photo credits: Cover and page 1, ©Irochka/Dreamstime.com; page 5,
©iStockphoto.com/JLBarranco; page 8, ©liewwk, used under license
from Shutterstock, Inc.; page 12, ©iStockphoto.com/JLFCapture; page
16, ©iStockphoto.com/WAS_; page 17, ©Dolnikov, used under license
from Shutterstock, Inc.; page 20, ©WILDLIFE GmbH/Alamy; page 24,
©OJO Images Ltd/Alamy; page 28, ©Andrew Darrington/Alamy

Library of Congress Cataloging-in-Publication Data
Gray, Susan Heinrichs.
  Super cool science experiments: Bugs / by Susan H. Gray.
    p. cm.—(Science explorer)
  Includes bibliographical references and index.
  ISBN-13: 978-1-60279-521-1   ISBN-10: 1-60279-521-5 (lib. bdg.)
  ISBN-13: 978-1-60279-600-3   ISBN-10: 1-60279-600-9 (pbk.)
  1. Entomology—Experiments—Juvenile literature. 2. Insects—
Experiments—Juvenile literature. I. Title. II. Title: Bugs. III. Series.
  QL467.2.G725 2009
  595.7078—dc22   2009006007

Cherry Lake Publishing would like to acknowledge the work
of The Partnership for 21st Century Skills. Please visit
www.21stcenturyskills.org for more information.

BUGS

TABLE OF CONTENTS

A Creepy, Crawly Classroom

Are there bugs living in your school? Have you seen spiderwebs in the hallway? Or a ladybug under your desk? How about flies in the cafeteria? Has a bee been buzzing through your classroom? If so, you might have thought they were pests. Soon you'll see that a school may not be such a strange place for bugs. That's because bugs make great teachers!

Have you ever wondered why bugs act the way they do? Or why bugs like living in certain places but not others? If so, you are on your way to thinking like a scientist. In this book, we'll look at bugs the way scientists do. We'll do that by experimenting with bugs and worms. Did you know that you can do experiments with things you already have at home? As we work, we'll learn how scientists think. We'll also learn how bugs "think," and we'll see what they can teach us as we design our own experiments. Don't forget the best part: we'll have lots of fun along the way!

First Things First

Calling all entomologists in training!

Scientists learn by studying things in nature very carefully. For example, scientists who study insects are called entomologists. These scientists look at how insects behave. They see which bugs live alone and which ones live in colonies. They study bugs that destroy crops and look for ways to stop them.

Scientists know that even though we're calling our creeping crawlers "bugs," there is a difference between insects, worms, bugs, spiders, and other tiny critters. Insects have six legs and three body parts. They also usually have two antennae and four wings. So worms are not insects. Bugs are specific types of insects. They have mouths shaped like straws. Spiders belong in a different category because they have different features. These include having eight legs and two body parts.

Good scientists take notes on everything they discover. They write down their observations. Sometimes those observations lead scientists to ask new questions. With new questions in mind, they design experiments to find the answers.

When scientists design experiments, they must think very clearly. The way they think about problems is often called the scientific method. What is the scientific method? It's a step-by-step way of finding answers to specific questions. The steps don't always follow the same pattern. Sometimes scientists change their minds. The process often works something like this:

Scientific method

- **Step One:** A scientist gathers the facts and makes observations about one particular thing.
- **Step Two:** The scientist comes up with a question that is not answered by all the observations and facts.

- **Step Three:** The scientist creates a hypothesis. This is a statement of what the scientist thinks is probably the answer to the question.
- **Step Four:** The scientist tests the hypothesis. He or she designs an experiment to see whether the hypothesis is correct. The scientist does the experiment and writes down what happens.
- **Step Five:** The scientist draws a conclusion based on how the experiment turned out. The conclusion might be that the hypothesis is correct. Sometimes, though, the hypothesis is not correct. In that case, the scientist might develop a new hypothesis and another experiment.

In the following experiments, we'll see the scientific method in action. We'll gather some facts and observations about bugs and worms. Then we'll develop some questions and a hypothesis. Next, we'll do an experiment to see if our hypothesis is correct. By the end of the experiment, we should know something new about bugs or worms. Okay, scientists! Let's get to work in our creepy, crawly laboratory!

Experiment #1
Damp or Dry?

← Have you ever seen a roly-poly bug?

Before we do any experiments, we should gather some observations. Our first two experiments will deal with roly-poly bugs. Some people call them pill bugs or sow bugs. Because of their features, scientists call them isopods. Different types of isopods live on land or in water.

Roly-poly bugs roll up in a ball when they sense danger. You may have seen them outside, next to the foundation of your home or under rocks in a garden. Since you'll need to find some of these little bugs, go outside and turn over some large rocks. Do you see any there? Try looking under old logs or flowerpots. These same spots at a park might be a good place to find them, too. Always be very gentle when you pick them up. It may be easier to scoop them up with a spoon than to use your fingers. You can keep the bugs in a margarine tub with some damp soil, tree bark, and crushed leaves. Ask an adult to poke some small airholes in the tub's lid. Then keep the lid on the tub.

As you collect your bugs, observe the places where they seem to be found the most. Are these dark places or brightly lit places? Warm or cool places? Damp or dry places? Do you think it matters to these isopods where they live? Or do you think that anyplace is fine with them?

These questions, along with our observations, lead us to create a hypothesis. Let's focus on moisture for this hypothesis. Here is one possibility: **Roly-polies would rather be in damp places than in dry ones.** Do this experiment in a room that has low, even lighting and no air currents. You don't want the light or any breezes to influence how your bugs act.

Here's what you'll need:

- 8–10 crushed dead leaves
- Dry wood chips or pieces of tree bark. Garden mulch should work well, but make sure it is made of plant material and has not been treated with chemicals or dyes.
- 2 handfuls of dry soil
- Water
- A cookie sheet
- 10 roly-polies

Let's get our hands dirty!

Instructions:

1. Mix the dead leaves, wood chips, and soil together.
2. Divide the mixture into 2 equal heaps.
3. Add enough water to 1 heap to make it very damp. Work this heap between your hands to make sure the moisture is spread evenly.
4. Set the cookie sheet on a flat surface.
5. Place the damp heap at 1 end of the cookie sheet, and place the dry heap at the other end. Pat the heaps a bit with your hand, to flatten them slightly and spread them out.

6. Release the roly-poly bugs into the middle of the cookie sheet between the 2 mounds. Try your best to place them in the center of the sheet, so that they are the same distance from both heaps.

7. For the next 20 minutes, observe their behavior. As you watch them, be sure you are not breathing on them.

In this experiment, you were warned not to use materials that had been treated with chemicals. Do you think chemicals might have changed the way the bugs acted? How might you have drawn the wrong conclusion if chemicals were involved? For one thing, the roly-poly bugs probably would not want to be near the treated mulch. Plus, the chemicals in treated mulch could hurt or even kill them. That is the last thing you want to happen!

Conclusion:

After 20 minutes, how many bugs made their way to the damp mound? How many ended up in the dry one? How many were still wandering around the cookie sheet? Did any roly-polies try one mound first and then the other? If so, what does this tell you about which mound the roly-polies prefer? Was your hypothesis correct? What is your conclusion?

Roly-polies breathe through special structures that are similar to fish gills. These gill-like structures are on the underside of their bodies. They must stay moist in order for the bugs to breathe. Does this help explain why these bugs prefer damp places?

Experiment #2

Are Bugs Bugged by Light?

When you collected bugs for the first experiment, you observed the kinds of places where they lived. They seemed to prefer damp spots, and your first experiment probably showed that to be true. Did you also notice whether the bugs preferred dark spots or brightly lit spots? Let's do an experiment to find out for sure. Choose one of these two hypotheses:

Hypothesis #1: Pill bugs prefer the dark.

Hypothesis #2: Pill bugs prefer bright light.

Here's what you'll need:

- 2–4 paper towels
- Water
- A cookie sheet
- A large sheet of black construction paper or black plastic. A sheet cut from a black plastic garbage bag should work.
- Tape
- A lamp that produces bright light
- 10 roly-polies

Make sure you have everything you need before you begin.

Instructions:

1. Wet the paper towels with water.
2. Lay the paper towels out flat on the cookie sheet. The paper towels should completely cover it.
3. Cover the left one-third of the cookie sheet with the black paper or plastic, as if you were wrapping a present. Tape the edges to the cookie sheet so that it stays in place. There should be a bit of space between the black paper or plastic and the surface of the damp paper towels.

Notes

Helpful Hint: Set a timer for 10 minutes to help you remember to make your observations.

4. Set the cookie sheet next to the lamp. The right side of the sheet (the side without the paper or plastic) should be closest to the lamp.
5. Turn the lamp on. The cookie sheet should now have a brightly lit side and a shaded side.
6. Place the roly-polies on the center of the cookie sheet.
7. Observe their behavior for the next hour. Every 10 minutes, check how many are in the dark area and how many are in the lit area. Write down what you see.

Conclusion:

By the end of your experiment, were more roly-polies in the dark area or bright area? Does this seem to suggest that the roly-polies prefer one area over the other? Was your hypothesis correct? What is your conclusion?

Bugs have nutrients that birds need.

Roly-polies eat rotting plant and animal matter. Birds will often eat *them*. Think about it. When do you think roly-polies go out looking for food—during the day or at night? Why?

Experiment #3 Smelly Old Worms

↖ Humans use their noses to smell.

How do you smell? Is that a rude question? If so, it wasn't meant to be. When you smell things, you are detecting certain chemicals in the air. They enter your nostrils and eventually reach special cells deep inside your nose. These cells send signals to the brain about the chemicals. The brain interprets those signals as different smells.

That's how we smell things. But what about other animals such as bugs and worms? Can they smell things? Can they also pick up chemicals in the air? Let's do an experiment to find out. We'll see if worms can sense chemicals. What do you think? Here's one hypothesis you might want to test: **Worms can sense chemicals in their environment.**

Here's what you'll need:

- 2 moist heaps of soil, each containing about 3 cups of soil. Each mound should be about the size of a grapefruit.
- A shallow plastic box at least 10 inches (25.4 centimeters) wide and at least 16 inches (40.6 cm) long
- A water or medicine dropper
- Ammonia
- 5 earthworms. You can buy them from a bait shop or pet store. You can also probably find them easily in damp soil.

Be careful when you work with ammonia.

Ammonia

Instructions:

1. Place the moist heaps of soil at opposite ends inside the plastic box.
2. Fill the dropper with ammonia. Always be very careful when using ammonia. Do not get any in your eyes.
3. Add 30 drops of ammonia to 1 of the heaps.
4. Place the worms in the center of the box. Observe the worms for the next 15 minutes, and write down what you see.

Conclusion:

What do you notice about the worms' behavior? Do they seem to prefer one mound over another? Did any worms move into the ammonia heap? How many moved into the other heap? Did any worms just do nothing? What do your findings suggest about the worms' ability to sense chemicals? Was the hypothesis correct?

Earthworms may not have nostrils, but they do have sensors on their bodies. When the sensors detect harmful chemicals in the soil, the worms move away. If you dumped a cleaning solution containing ammonia onto the ground, what do you think the worms in the soil would do?

Experiment #4

Mealworms and Magnets

← Mealworms change form as they mature into beetles.

You've seen that bugs and worms respond to light, moisture, and chemicals. But there are many other things that might affect their activity. In fact, scientists believe that some insects respond to magnetic fields. Honeybees are one type of insect whose movements can be affected by Earth's magnetic field. Could the same be true for mealworms? In this experiment, we'll find out whether mealworms respond to magnetism. Think of a hypothesis that relates to magnets and the behavior of mealworms. Here's one option: **Mealworms will move toward magnets.**

Here's what you'll need:
- 10–15 small magnets. You can find these at hobby and craft stores. You can also find them at discount stores in the craft section.
- A dinner plate
- 24 mealworms. You can find these at a pet store or bait shop. They should be kept in a container with food and airholes. You may keep the container in the refrigerator until you're ready to start the experiment.

Get ready to experiment!

Instructions:

1. Place the magnets end to end around the rim of half of the plate. Leave the other half of the plate without magnets. The group of magnets should form a C shape if you look at the plate from above.
2. Place 8 of the mealworms in the very center of the plate.
3. Observe the worms for the next 10 minutes. Every 2 minutes, write down how many worms have made their way to the half of the plate with magnets. Also record how many are on the half without magnets.
4. Try this experiment 2 more times. Each time, use a different group of 8 mealworms.

Observe each group of mealworms carefully.

Conclusion:

Which half of the plate has more mealworms by the end of each 10-minute period? Does it seem that the mealworms are clearly drawn to the magnets? Or do the mealworms seem to be moving about the plate in no particular order or pattern? Was the hypothesis correct?

Sometimes, experiments turn out differently from what everyone expects. When this happens, scientists say that the experiments ended with negative results. The magnetic mealworm experiment is one such example. Magnets did not seem to affect the mealworms' movements at all. Our hypothesis was incorrect. Do you think experiments ending in negative results are a waste of time? Why or why not? Actually, the results of an experiment are always valuable. You can almost always learn something from an experiment— even when the hypothesis is incorrect.

Experiment #5

Which Worms Wiggle Wildly?

Why are some kids faster than others? Do you think some worms are faster for the same reasons?

In the last experiment, you observed the movement of mealworms. Some worms probably were speedy crawlers, while others moved slowly. What might cause some worms to move slowly and some quickly? Could it have something to do with their age or their size? Could their temperature have an effect? Let's do an experiment to find out. Focus on temperature and speed. Have you thought of a hypothesis? Try this one: **Warm worms move more quickly than cold worms.**

Here's what you'll need:
- A coffee mug
- 2 identical dinner plates or pie pans
- A marking pen with washable ink
- An adult helper
- 2 margarine tubs with lids
- 20 mealworms
- A cold place, such as a refrigerator
- A warm place, such as a sunny windowsill

Your kitchen can be a great place to experiment.

Instructions:

1. Place the coffee mug upside down in the center of the plate or pie pan.

2. Trace around the rim of the mug using the marking pen. When you are finished, you should have drawn a nearly perfect circle in the center of the plate or pan.

3. Repeat steps 1 and 2 with the other plate or pie pan.

4. Have an adult poke some small airholes in the lids of the margarine tubs.

5. Carefully place 10 mealworms in each tub. Cover the tubs with the lids.

6. Put 1 tub and 1 plate in a refrigerator or another cold place for 20 minutes. Do not use a freezer!

7. Put the other tub and plate on a sunny windowsill or in another warm spot for 20 minutes.

8. After 20 minutes, place the cooled and warmed plates side by side in a spot that is not in direct sunlight.

9. Very carefully—but quickly—dump the cold worms out of the tub and inside the circle on the cold plate.

Who knew your refrigerator could be a science tool?

FOR MORE INFORMATION

BOOKS

Backyard Laboratory. New York: Scholastic, 2008.

Davies, Andrew. *Super-Size Bugs.* New York: Sterling Publishing, 2008.

Hardyman, Robyn. *Bugs.* Redding, CT: Brown Bear Books, 2009.

WEB SITES

Discovery Kids—Put Some Worms to Work

yucky.discovery.com/flash/fun_n_games/ activities/activities/activity_worms.html

For a fun project with worms

PBS Kids—ZOOMsci: Counting Bugs

pbskids.org/zoom/activities/sci/countingbugs. html

Try a simple activity that will help you learn about bugs in your area

Sacramento Zoo—Mealworm to Beetle Project

www.saczoo.com/Page.aspx?pid=441

Learn how to set up a home for mealworms, and watch them grow and develop

INDEX

About the → Author

Susan H. Gray has a master's degree in zoology. She has written more than 100 science and reference books for children and especially loves writing about biology. Susan also likes to garden and play the piano. She lives in Cabot, Arkansas, with her husband, Michael, and many pets.